THE MOST FAMOUS INVENTORS WHO EVER LIVED

Inventor's Guide

Children's Inventors Books

Speedy Publishing LLC
40 E. Main St. #1156
Newark, DE 19711
www.speedypublishing.com
Copyright 2017

All Rights reserved. No part of this book may be reproduced or used in any way or form or by any means whether electronic or mechanical, this means that you cannot record or photocopy any material ideas or tips that are provided in this book

An invention may start with a dream, or with a thought about how to make life better. But somebody has to dream that dream or have that thought. That person may be an inventor! Let's find out about some of the greatest inventors ever.

WHAT INVENTORS HAVE IN COMMON

Inventors work in many different areas, from farming to sailing ships, from working behind a desk to working on an assembly line. They see something that is dangerous or slow or not efficient, and start to think about how to make that thing work better.

A lot of the ideas and experiments go nowhere, but some lead to new discoveries that can change the way we live.

nventors are agents of change. Here are some of the common characteristics they share:

- They don't give up if their first attempt, or even their first one hundred attempts, does not succeed.
- They care deeply about what they are doing.
- They are willing to ignore comments like "that's how we always do it" and "it will never work."
- They have vivid imaginations: they can dream how things might be.

- They take risks.
- They have a good sense of humor, and are not afraid to seem foolish.

- **They embrace failure for what it can teach them.**
- **They can see the big problem and the details of its solution at the same time.**

- They can explain their ideas to other people.
- Solving problems in a neat way excites them.

THE FIRST FLIGHT OF AN AIRPLANE, THE WRIGHT FLYER ON DECEMBER 17, 1903

EARLY INVENTORS

ARCHIMEDES (287-212 BCE)

He was a Greek engineer, mathematician, astronomer, and inventor. He discovered the value of the mathematical constant ϖ, and designed the "Archimedes screw" to raise water from a lower to a higher level. Learn more about him in the Baby Professor book Archimedes and his Numbers.

ARCHIMEDES

CAI LUN (50–121 CE)

He invented ways of making paper from bark, hemp, silk, and even strands of old fishing nets!

GALILEO GALILEI, 1636

INVENTORS OF THE RENAISSANCE

GALILEO (1564-1642)

He established theories about gravity, the rotation of the Earth, and the nature of our solar system. He improved early designs of telescopes and compasses.

THOMAS SAVERY (1650-1715)

He invented one of the first steam engines to help pump water out of mine shafts.

JETHRO TULL (1674-1741)

In England, Tull invented the seed drill to improve seeding fields, and the horse-drawn hoe to improve weeding. His inventions greatly improved crop yields.

JOHN HARRISON (1693-1776)

He was a carpenter and clock-maker. He invented a device for measuring longitude (where you are east or west of your starting point; latitude tells you where you are north or south). This made navigation much easier and sailing much safer.

JOHN HARRISON

BENJAMIN FRANKLIN

INVENTORS OF THE MODERN AGE

BENJAMIN FRANKLIN (1705-1790)

As well as being an American politician, writer, and diplomat, Franklin was renowned scientist and inventor. He experimented with electricity, and invented the lightning rod, the Franklin stove, and bifocal glasses.

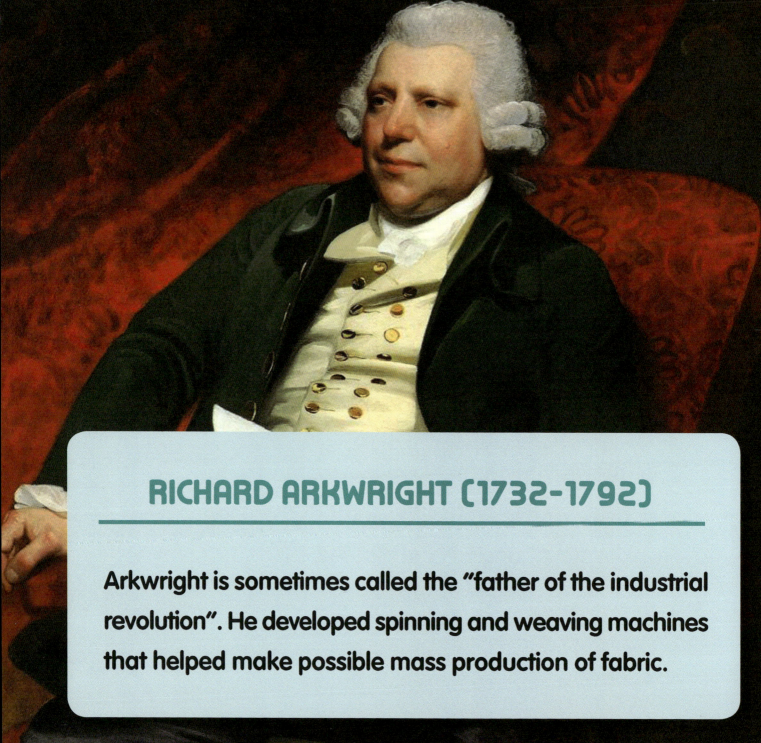

RICHARD ARKWRIGHT (1732-1792)

Arkwright is sometimes called the "father of the industrial revolution". He developed spinning and weaving machines that helped make possible mass production of fabric.

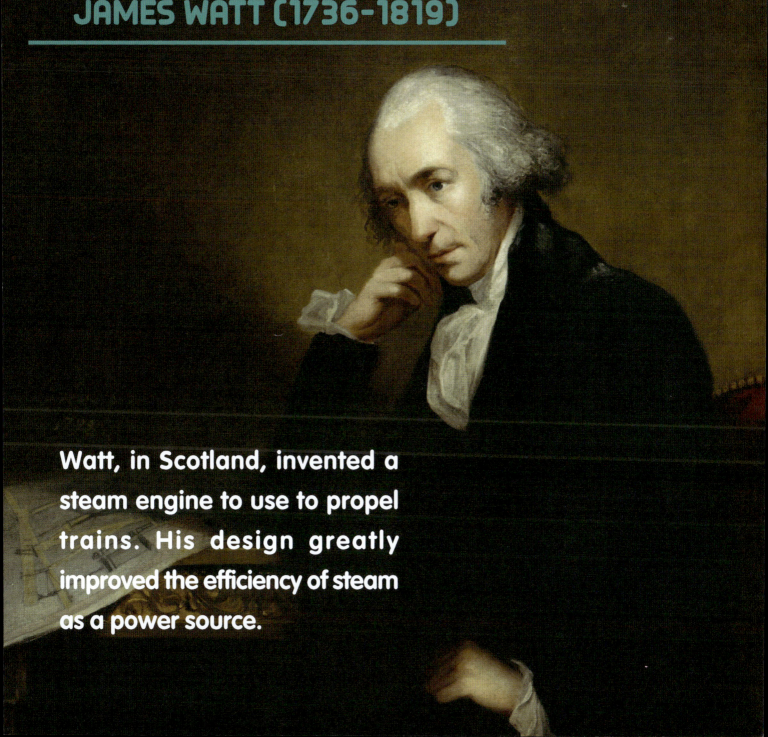

JAMES WATT (1736-1819)

Watt, in Scotland, invented a steam engine to use to propel trains. His design greatly improved the efficiency of steam as a power source.

CHARLES BABBAGE (1791-1871)

Babbage is considered the "father of computers". He designed the first mechanical computer.

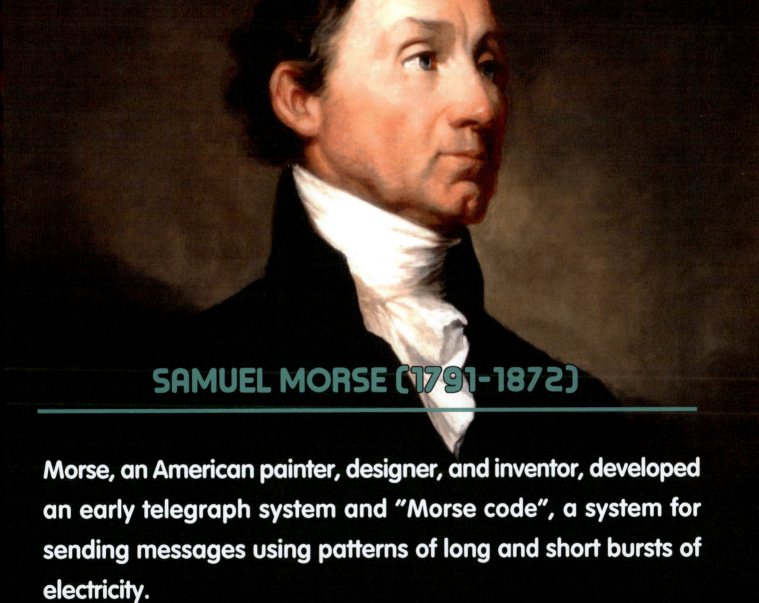

SAMUEL MORSE (1791-1872)

Morse, an American painter, designer, and inventor, developed an early telegraph system and "Morse code", a system for sending messages using patterns of long and short bursts of electricity.

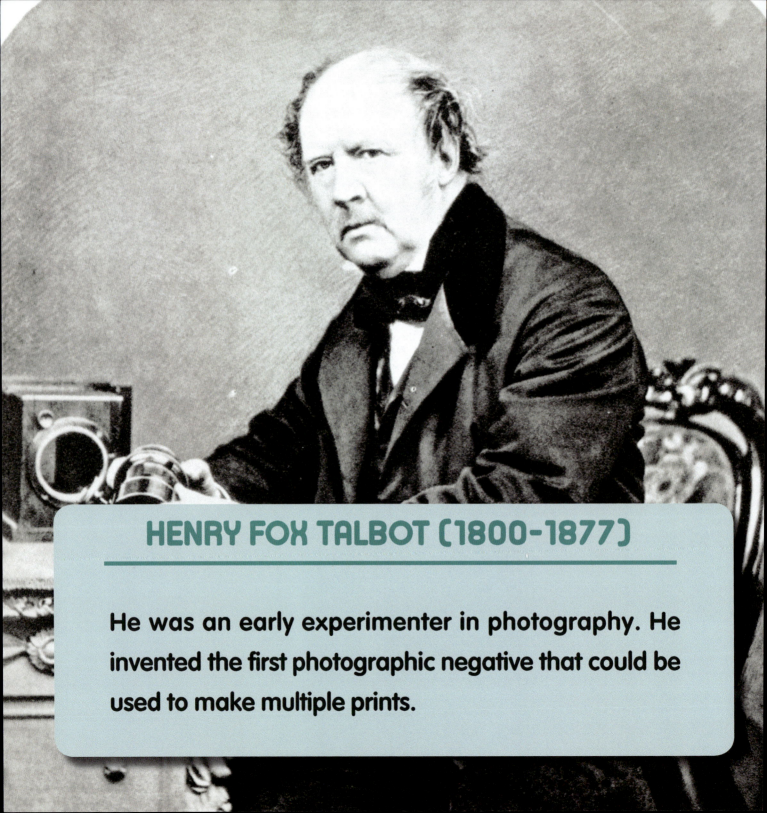

HENRY FOX TALBOT (1800-1877)

He was an early experimenter in photography. He invented the first photographic negative that could be used to make multiple prints.

LOUIS BRAILLE (1800-1852)

Braille lost his sight as a result of an accident as a child. He developed the Braille writing system of patterns of raised dots that allow blind people to read with their fingertips.

KIRKPATRICK MACMILLAN (1812-1878)

Macmillan invented the pedal bicycle, adding the chain system that lets the peddling motion provide energy to the rear wheel. This gave the bicycle the modern form we are familiar with.

JAMES CLERK MAXWELL (1831-1879)

Maxwell is best known for being one of the world's best physicists, but he also developed the first process for producing color photographs.

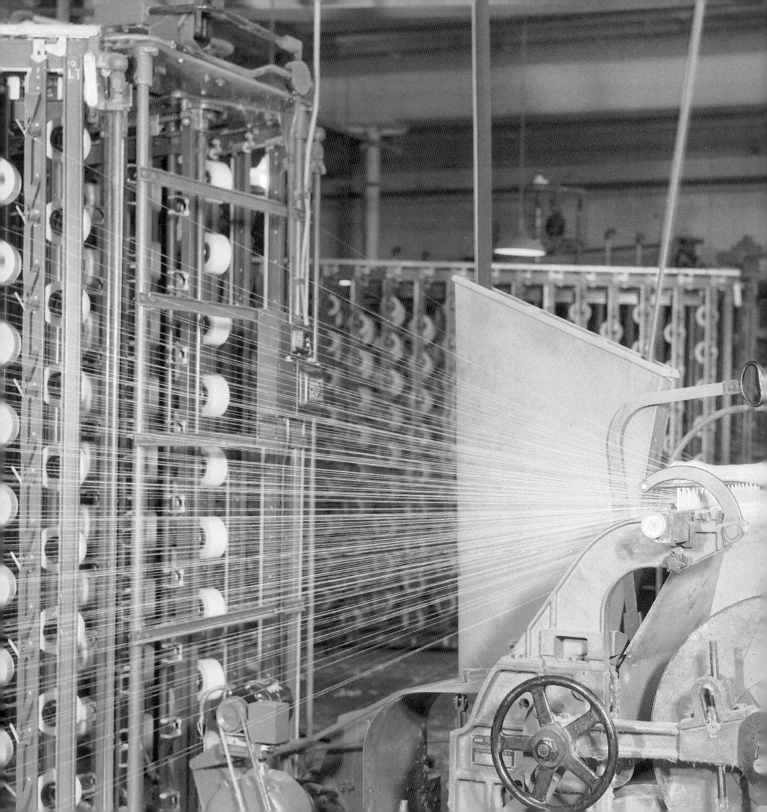

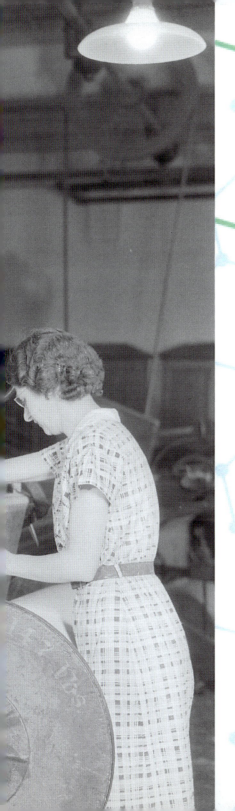

MARGARET KNIGHT (1838-1914)

Many of Knights inventions came from what she saw of dangerous conditions in factories, like the New Hampshire textile mill where she worked as a girl. She developed safety devices, machines to automatically perform repetitive tasks, and both rotary and piston driven engines. She received 27 patents and was sometimes called "the woman Edison".

KARL BENZ (1844-1929)

Benz, in Germany, developed the first gasoline-powered gas engine in 1879. This became the gateway discovery for the whole automobile industry.

THOMAS EDISON (1847-1931)

In his lifetime, Edison filed over one thousand patents. He developed an amazing array of products, from the electric light bulb to the phonograph and the motion picture camera. He was one of the greatest inventors in history.

ALEXANDER GRAHAM BELL
(1847-1922)

Bell worked in many fields, including airplane design, hydrofoil ships, and telecommunications, including video phones. He invented the first telephone system suitable for everyday use.

NIKOLA TESLA (1856-1943)

Tesla was an accomplished physicist. He invented florescent lighting, three-phase electricity, alternating current, and many groundbreaking electrical devices.

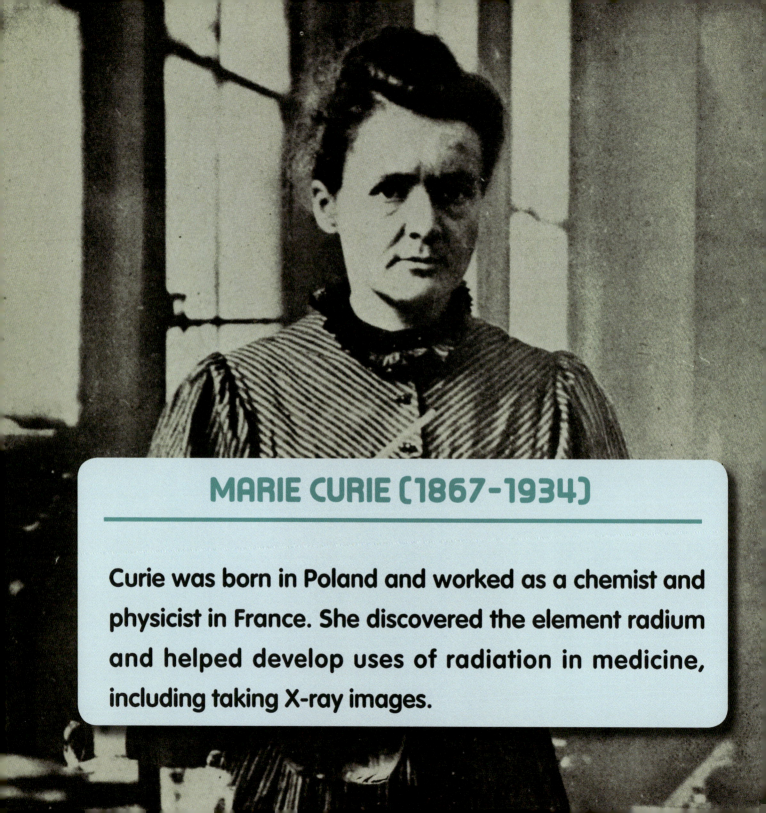

MARIE CURIE (1867-1934)

Curie was born in Poland and worked as a chemist and physicist in France. She discovered the element radium and helped develop uses of radiation in medicine, including taking X-ray images.

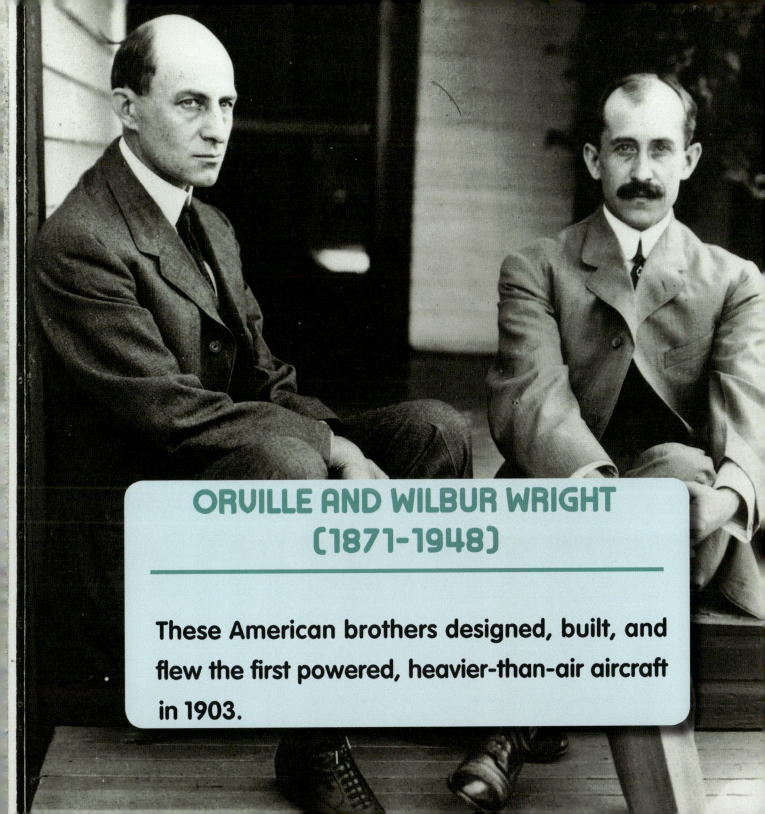

ORVILLE AND WILBUR WRIGHT
(1871-1948)

These American brothers designed, built, and flew the first powered, heavier-than-air aircraft in 1903.

MELITTA BENTZ (1873-1950)

Bentz, a German housewife, invented a filter system for making coffee that removed grit and bitterness from the drink. Coffee had been brewed since at least the eleventh century, but the liquid was much rougher than what we expect today. Bentz developed a filter involving absorbent paper with some holes punched through it.

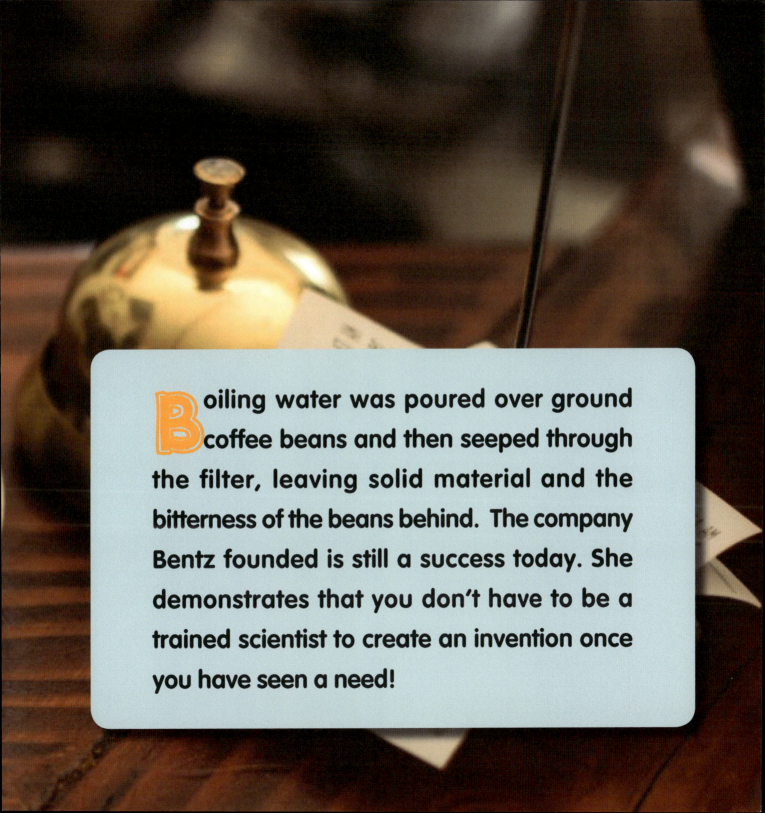

Boiling water was poured over ground coffee beans and then seeped through the filter, leaving solid material and the bitterness of the beans behind. The company Bentz founded is still a success today. She demonstrates that you don't have to be a trained scientist to create an invention once you have seen a need!

ALEXANDER FLEMING (1881-1955)

Fleming accidentally discovered penicillin, an important antibiotic that changed the prospects of many sick people, in 1928 while doing research on mould.

JOHN LOGIE BAIRD (1888-1946)

Baird, a Scot, invented the first television system, and the first device for recording television broadcasts.

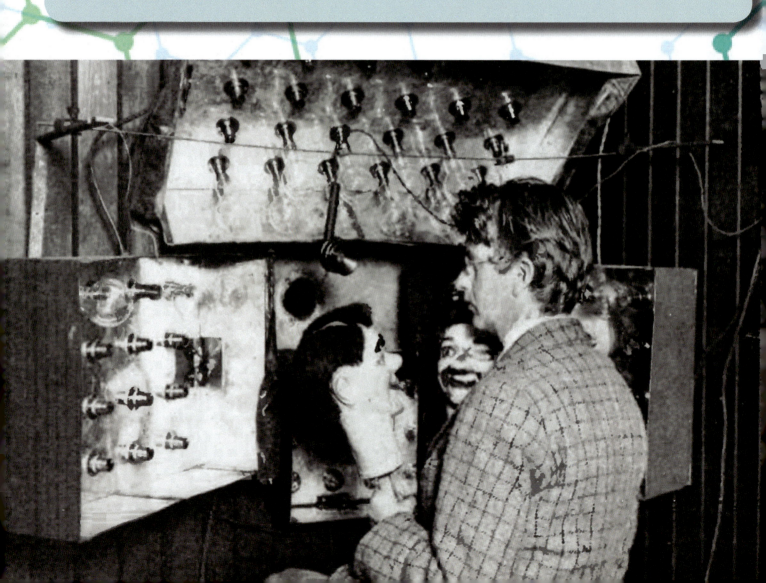

ENRICO FERMI (1901-1954)

Fermi made many discoveries in the field of radiation, and led development of the first nuclear reactor.

ROBERT OPPENHEIMER

ROBERT OPPENHEIMER (1904-1967)

Oppenheimer was the lead scientist on the Manhattan Project, the secret research effort during World War II. The result of the research was the atomic bomb, the most powerful weapon ever developed. Oppenheimer later led protests against the use of this weapon.

ALAN TURING (1912-1954)

Turing was an English mathematician. He worked on computer processes and the development of artificial intelligence. His "Turing Test" is a way of telling whether you are communicating with a human or with a machine.

STEPHANIE KWOLEK (1923-2014)

Kowlek was a chemist in the United States. She worked on developing synthetic fibers, and in 1965 discovered a very lightweight and durable polymer, a large molecular structure. This polymer could be generated into fiber, which could be woven into protective material. The new material, Kevlar, is used in protective equipment like helmets and bulletproof vests, work gloves, sports equipment, building materials, and the insulation of fiber-optic cables. Kwolek received the National Medal of Technology for her research.

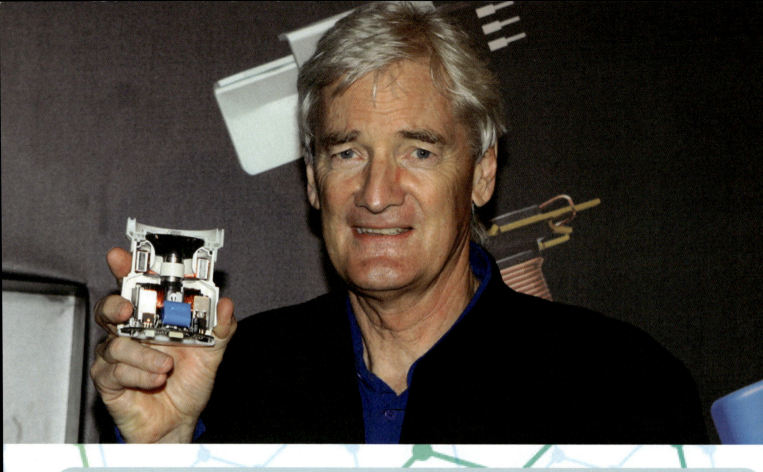

JAMES DYSON (1947-)

Dyson developed a vacuum cleaner that did not require a filter or a bag to keep from distributing the dust it collected back into the room. He also adapted his discoveries to create extremely powerful and efficient hand dryers.

TIM BERNERS-LEE (1955-)

Berners-Lee, a British computer scientist, is considered the creator of the World-Wide Web, the system that we use when we type an address in our computer browser to go to a website. He provided his discoveries and developments to the world at no cost.

STEVE JOBS (1955-2011)

Jobs was an American technology developer and business leader. He helped personal computing devices make huge steps forward, and the designs and interfaces of the devices he developed have influenced all other computer and mobile device designs. Jobs invented the concept and style of hand-held computing devices.

THE NEXT INVENTORS

Inventors see something that could be better. Then they try to figure out what would achieve "better". Each inventor starts from what those before have developed and carries things forward. All of the inventors in this book have set the stage for inventors of the future—maybe including you!

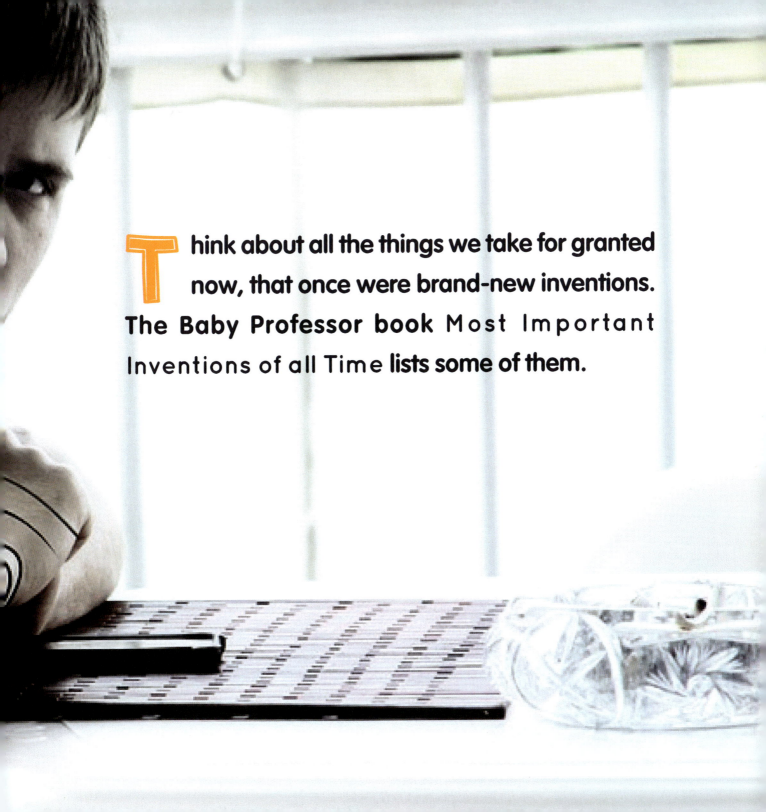

Think about all the things we take for granted now, that once were brand-new inventions. The Baby Professor book Most Important Inventions of all Time lists some of them.

Visit

Tech Tron
Computers & Technology

www.TechTron.com

to download Free Tech Tron eBooks and view our catalog of new and exciting Children's Books